It's a Dog's Life

by Mary Lindeen

Table of Contents

A Dog's Life 2

Working Dogs 4

Service Dogs 8

Best Friends 14

Glossary 16

Consultant:
Adria F. Klein, Ph.D.
California State University, San Bernardino

capstone
classroom

Heinemann Raintree • Red Brick Learning
division of Capstone

A Dog's Life

A dog's day is always busy. There are balls to chase and bones to chew. Many dogs spend their whole lives playing and sleeping.

Some dogs spend part of their days at work. These dogs have learned how to help people. Some of them go to special schools. Others are **trained** by their owners.

Working Dogs

This is a **herding dog**. He helps the farmer take care of the sheep.

The sheep roam all over looking for grass to eat. The dog keeps them from getting lost. He runs and barks at the sheep to keep them in the right spot.

This dog knows how to find a person lost in the woods. He uses his nose to pick up the person's **scent**. He barks when the person is found.

This dog also uses his **sense** of smell. He has a job too. He helps the police find criminals. He is trained to pick up a scent and follow it.

Service Dogs

Service dogs must be smart and gentle. Their training begins when they are puppies. They learn simple things, like how to sit and stay.

Then they go to special schools. Trainers teach them how to be **guide dogs** and **therapy dogs**. Then each dog is matched with the owner who is just right for them.

This is a hearing dog. He is trained to help a person who is deaf. The dog listens for the doorbell and other important sounds.

This dog is trained to help around the house. She can turn on lights and pick up clothes. Her special vest shows everyone when she is on the job.

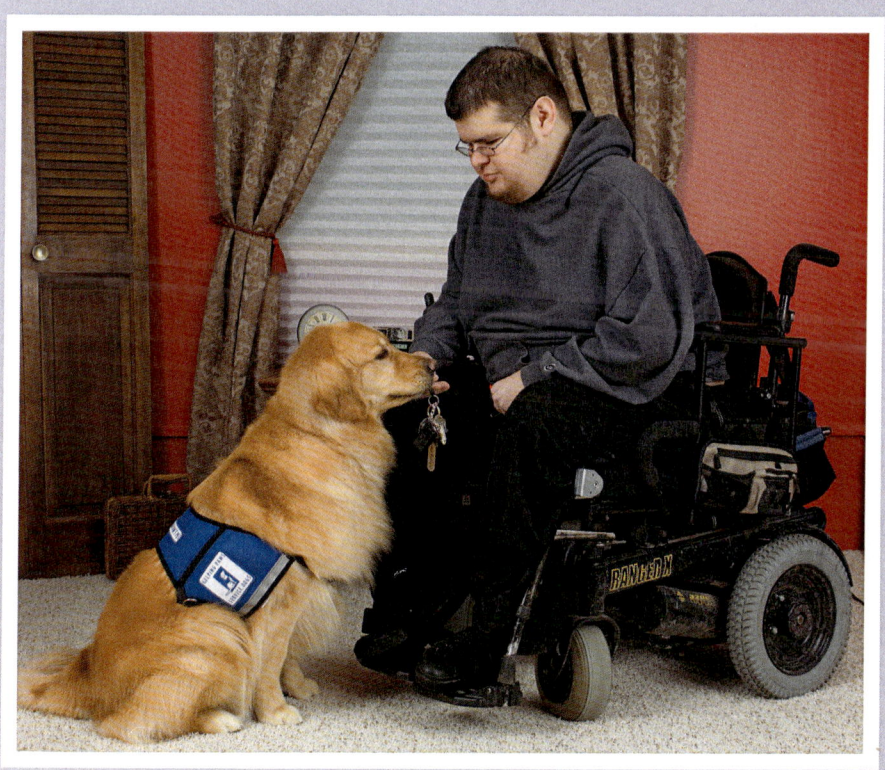

This guide dog helps a person who is blind. The person holds on to the dog's **harness**. This guide dog knows when it is safe to walk across the street.

This therapy dog visits hospitals and nursing homes. This dog helps to make people feel good.

Best Friends

Owners need to take good care of their dogs so they can work hard. Taking them for walks is important. Feeding them good food keeps them happy and healthy.

Dogs don't always have to work. They can have fun too. This dog is a best friend!

Glossary

guide dog   a dog that is trained to work with blind people

harness   a strap attached to a dog, with a handle for a person to hold

herding dog   a dog that gathers and looks after sheep or cattle

scent   a smell

sense   the ability to see, hear, smell, touch, or taste

therapy dog   a dog that is trained to give people comfort

train   to teach